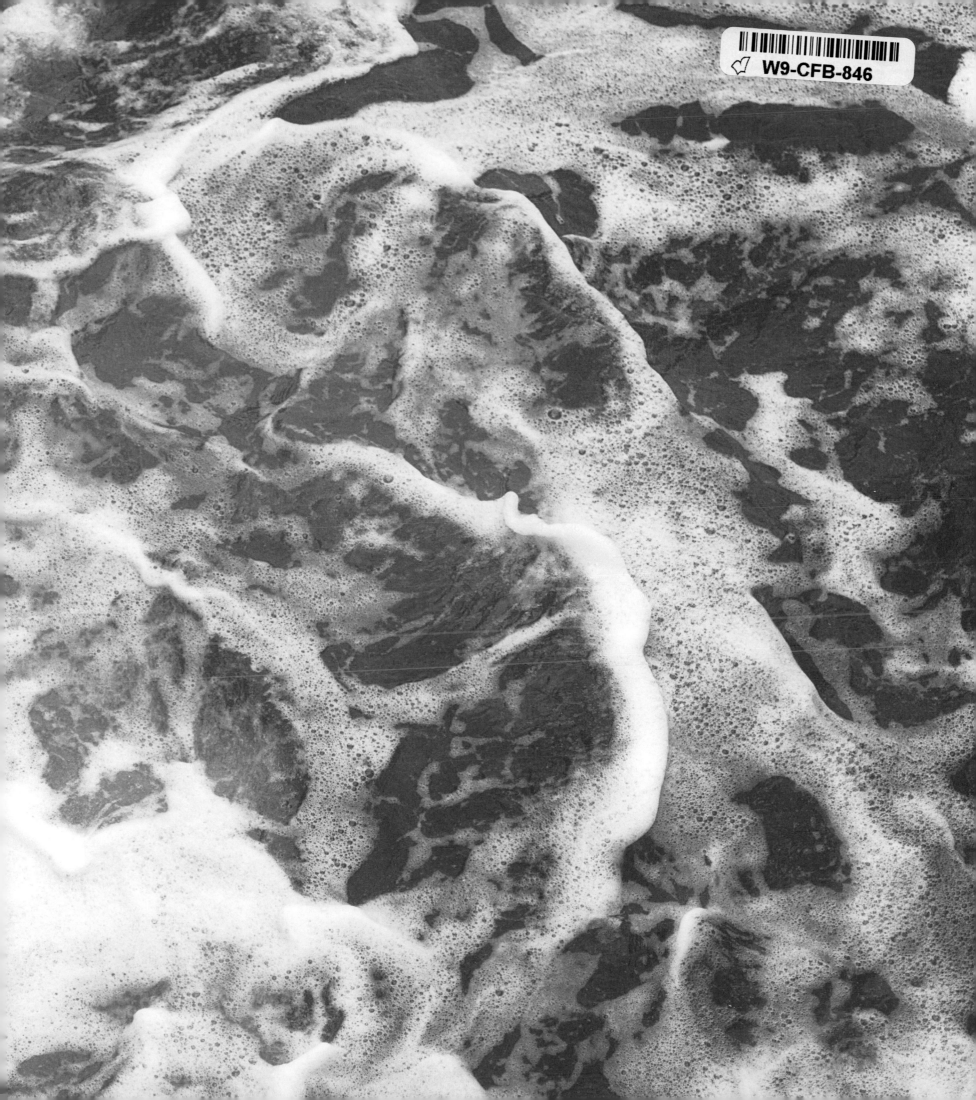

THE WONDER OF DOLPHINS

THE WONDER OF DOLPHINS

FOG CITY PRESS

Published by Fog City Press,
a division of Weldon Owen Inc.
1045 Sansome Street
San Francisco, CA 94111 USA

www.weldonowen.com

weldon**owen**

President & Publisher Roger Shaw
Associate Publisher Mariah Bear
SVP, Sales & Marketing Amy Kaneko
Finance Manager Philip Paulick
Editor Bridget Fitzgerald
Creative Director Kelly Booth
Art Director Meghan Hildebrand
Senior Production Designer Rachel Lopez Metzger
Production Director Chris Hemesath
Associate Production Director Michelle Duggan
Director of Enterprise Systems Shawn Macey
Imaging Manager Don Hill

Weldon Owen is a division of Bonnier Publishing.

Library of Congress Control Number on file with the publisher.

ISBN 13: 978-1-68188-121-8
ISBN 10: 1-68188-121-7

10 9 8 7 6 5 4 3 2 1

2016 2017 2018 2019

Printed by 1010 Printing in China.

Dolphins are some of the world's smartest animals. Most live in the ocean, but a few live in rivers. Dolphins are very sociable and playful—even adult dolphins have been seen playing with seaweed and sticks.

Most dolphins live in groups called pods. Dolphin babies live with their mothers until they are about six years old. Then they form new pods with other dolphins their own age.

Although dolphins live in water, they breathe air and have to come to the surface to breathe.

Fun Fact
Dolphins have great hearing and good eyesight.

Fun Fact

Baby dolphins are called calves.

A dolphin is
born underwater.
The mother then
helps the baby
swim to the
surface for air.

Fun Fact

Dolphins can hold
their breath for
7-15 minutes.

A dolphin breathes through a blowhole
on top of its head. The blowhole
closes underwater.

Dolphins are very smart and have large brains. They like to explore.

Fun Fact
Female dolphins are called cows. Males are called bulls.

Fun Fact

Some super-pods can have up to 1,000 dolphins.

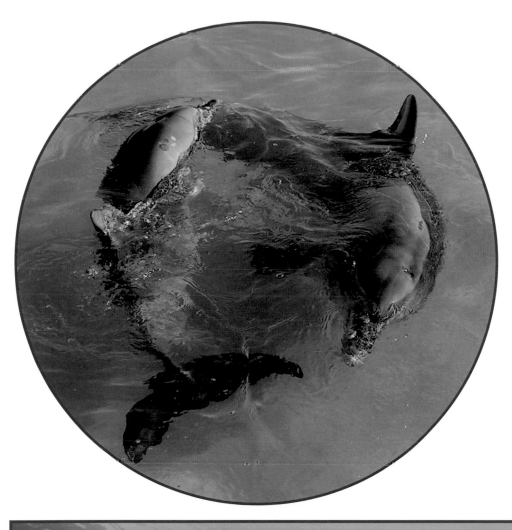

Dolphins are very social animals. You can often see them playing with other dolphins in their pod.

Sometimes dolphins look like they are leaping out of the water just for fun.

Fun Fact

Some dolphins can jump as high as 30 feet (9 m)!

Dolphins communicate with each other using clicks and whistles.

Fun Fact

Even with teeth,
dolphins swallow
their prey whole.

Fun Fact
Dolphins are meat-eaters, or carnivores.

Some dolphins work together to hunt fish. They also eat squid and crustaceans.

Dolphins may look like fish, but they are mammals. Mammals feed their babies milk and look after them.

Fun Fact
Echoes identify the exact size and shape of objects.

Dolphins can send out high-pitched sounds and use the echoes to navigate and find food. This process is called echolocation.

The shape of dolphins' bodies helps them swim really fast—up to 25 mph (40 kph)!

Fun Fact

Dolphins usually live about 17 years–or longer.

Fun Fact

A dolphin can eat 30 pounds (13 kg) of fish every day!

Some dolphins in the wild have been observed to live over 50 years!

Most dolphins live in the sea, where
they travel and hunt in groups.

Fun Fact

Dolphins are cetaceans (marine mammals).

Fun Fact
Boto dolphins live in South America's Amazon River.

Species include
southern right
whale dolphins
(below) and
Heaviside's
dolphins (left).

Orcas are often called killer whales, but they are actually the biggest dolphins in the world.

Fun Fact

An orca can grow to the size of a school bus!

Fun Fact
Harbor porpoises love to swim in shallow waters.

Porpoises are often confused with dolphins, but they are smaller and have rounded faces.

Fun Fact
Dolphins have helped
people in need.

Usually dolphins are not afraid of people.
They will sometimes swim with divers.

In some places, you can get close enough to dolphins to touch them.

Fun Fact

Dolphins can be gentle, but they are still wild animals!

Dolphins can be trained to do special activities. They practice some of the same skills they use in the wild, such as jumping.

Fun Fact

Bottlenose dolphins can perform complex tricks.

Fun Fact

Dolphins are found in seas and rivers worldwide!

You can see
dolphins up close
and learn more
about them at
the aquarium.
Dive in!